ORANGUTANS

Patricia Davis

J
599.883
D

Grolier
an imprint of

SCHOLASTIC

www.scholastic.com/librarypublishing

Published 2009 by Grolier
An imprint of Scholastic Library Publishing
Old Sherman Turnpike, Danbury,
Connecticut 06816

For The Brown Reference Group plc
Project Editor: Jolyon Goddard
Picture Researcher: Clare Newman
Designers: Dave Allen, Jeni Child, Lynne Ross,
          Sarah Williams
Managing Editors: Bridget Giles, Tim Harris

Volume ISBN-13: 978-0-7172-8030-8
Volume ISBN-10: 0-7172-8030-6

Library of Congress
Cataloging-in-Publication Data

Nature's children. Set 4.
    p. cm.
  Includes bibliographical references and
  index.
  ISBN 13: 978-0-7172-8083-4
  ISBN 10: 0-7172-8083-7 ((set 4) : alk. paper)
  1. Animals--Encyclopedias, Juvenile. 1.
  Grolier (Firm)
  QL49.N385 2009
  590.3--dc22
                          2007046315

Printed and bound in China

Contents

FACT FILE: Orangutans

Class	Mammals (Mammalia)
Order	Lemurs, tarsiers, monkeys, and apes (Primates)
Family	Orangutans, gorillas, chimpanzees, and humans (Hominidae)
Genus	Orangutans (*Pongo*)
Species	Bornean orangutan (*Pongo pygmaeus*) and Sumatran orangutan (*P. abelii*)
World distribution	The islands of Borneo and Sumatra, in Southeast Asia
Habitat	Rain forests
Distinctive physical characteristics	Long fur, which may be reddish-brown or darker; both sexes have throat sacs and males grow fleshy cheek flaps; arms nearly twice as long as legs
Habits	Adults are solitary; spend most of the time in trees; build nests to sleep in
Diet	Mainly fruit but might also include other foods such as bark, leaves, mushrooms, nuts, honey, soil, insects, and small mammals

Introduction

Orangutans are shaggy-haired apes that are related to chimpanzees, gorillas, and humans. Until recently, little was known about orangutans because they live deep in the **rain forest**, away from humans. Orangutans are clever and fascinating animals. They are capable of making tools and remembering difficult routes through the forest. Many scientists now believe that these apes are more intelligent than chimpanzees.

The word *orangutan* is Malay for "person of the forest."

Orangutans are
the largest tree-
living animals in
the world.

Forest Dwellers

A long time ago, orangutans lived in many places in Asia. Today, however, they are found on just two islands in Southeast Asia: Borneo and Sumatra. Orangutans live deep in the tropical rain forests of these islands. These two groups of orangutans separated so long ago that they are now considered different types, or **species**—Bornean orangutans and Sumatran orangutans.

The rain forest is hot and steamy all year round, with little change between seasons. The average temperature is 86°F (30°C) during the day and 68°F (20°C) during the night—that's hot! In addition, there are heavy rain showers each day, usually in the afternoon. When there is a downpour, orangutans like to cover their head with giant leaves. They use these leaves like humans would use an umbrella.

Orangutans share the rain forests with thousands of other animals and plants, including strange-looking fruits, giant butterflies, and flying snakes!

In the Trees

Orangutans spend nearly all their time in the trees. In fact, they are the most **arboreal**, or tree-dwelling, of all the **great apes**. These great apes include gorillas, orangutans, chimps, and humans. Adult orangutans prefer to stay about halfway up trees, but lighter and more adventurous youngsters often climb into the treetops.

Orangutans are heavy animals. An adult male can weigh up to 165 pounds (75 kg)—about the same as an average adult human male. Adult females are about half that weight. Often, even the toughest branches crack under the strain of their weight. Sometimes, orangutans fall and injure themselves.

Despite their size, orangutans are well built for life in the trees. Their arms are nearly twice as long as their legs and perfect for swinging from branch to branch. They also have long, strong, hook-shaped fingers and toes—just right for gripping branches tightly.

An orangutan has very
flexible shoulder and hip
joints that allow its limbs
to move in many directions.

Orangutans spend up to 10 hours every day sleeping and resting in their nests.

Ready for Bed

Every night before going to sleep, orangutans build a large leafy nest. Just before sunset—which is orangutan bedtime—an orangutan finds a suitable location in a tree to build its nest. That might be a strong branch or a fork in the tree. The ape then gathers branches, bending and weaving them to make a firm base. For comfort, the orangutan pads the base with more twigs or leaves. Finally, it makes a roof by placing leaves and twigs on overhanging branches. This whole process takes about six minutes.

Once the nest is complete, it is time for bed. Orangutans sleep on their side or back, sometimes with one of their hands under their head, like a sleeping human. Most orangutans make a new nest every day. Sometimes, they return to an old nest for a nap during the day or to dodge a rainstorm.

Orangutan Hats

Orangutans love to put just about anything on their head. When it rains, they will cover it with large leaves. Even if it's not raining, orangutans happily pile twigs on their head. Some scientists think that this activity might help keep away stinging insects.

In the United States, some orangutans **in captivity** have been taught **sign language**. Sign language was invented to allow deaf people to communicate with hand signals or "signs." Orangutans learn the sign for "hat" faster than any other sign—even the sign for food! Orangutans that have been adopted by humans have been seen putting anything from saucepans to kittens on their head!

A young orangutan from Sumatra shelters under a giant leaf.

Because an orangutan's hands are very similar to a human's hands scientists have been able to teach them sign language.

Language Skills

Orangutans in captivity have been very successful in learning sign language. Chantek, a male orangutan in Zoo Atlanta, has learned about 150 different signs and can put them together to make sentences. He uses signs to plan ahead and will even "tell" lies to try to get his own way!

Another orangutan raised at the University of Tennessee uses a sign meaning "dirty" when he wants to go to the bathroom. He also uses this sign to trick his owners into letting him go to the bathroom to play with soap!

At the National Zoo in Washington, D.C., orangutans are learning to communicate in a sign language that has been designed especially for them. This project is known as the Orangutan Language Project.

Shaggy Coat

Orangutans are famous for their distinctive shaggy coat. They have matted tufts of long reddish-brown hair that help keep their skin dry during the frequent rain showers in the forest.

Youngsters usually have a bright orange coat that darkens with age. Not all adult orangutans are reddish-brown, however. Some adults in Borneo have brown or black hair. Sumatran orangutans have longer hair than their Bornean relatives, too.

Unlike chimpanzees and gorillas, which spend many hours each day **grooming** one another, orangutans do not seem to care how messy and matted their coat gets. In fact, most adult orangutans are such loners that they might not see another orangutan for a month or more. Perhaps that is the reason why they do not mind how messy they look!

A young Sumatran orangutan shows off his strong, hairy arms. Orangutans are about seven times stronger than human adults.

Adult males, such as this Bornean orangutan, are very unsociable. They only seek out the company of other orangutans during the mating season.

All By Myself

It takes a lot of food to fuel a body the size of an orangutan's. That might partly explain why orangutans are such loners. Orangutans mainly eat fruit, and fruit trees are widely scattered throughout the rain forest. If orangutans stayed together and ate from the same tree, there wouldn't be enough food for all of them. And because orangutans are slow movers, they probably wouldn't have time to visit enough trees each day. By the end of the day, they would be pretty hungry! For a lone orangutan, however, just one or two trees can provide enough fruit for one day.

Sometimes, several orangutans gather at a plentiful fruit tree. Surprisingly, they take little notice of one another and arrive, feed, and leave separately. Only the youngsters seem to enjoy one another's company. They play and tickle one another.

What's for Dinner?

The fruits orangutans eat include mangoes, plums, lychees (LIE-CHEEZ), rambutans (RAM-BEW-TANZ), and figs. They especially like a prickly, football-sized fruit called a **durian**. To a human nose, durians smell foul—like a mixture of moldy meat, rotten eggs, and old socks! Strangely enough, this stink does not seem to bother an orangutan. When an orangutan eats something that it finds delicious, it makes a huffing noise and smacks its lips noisily.

Orangutans eat a wide variety of other foods, too—about 400 in total. These include tree bark, mushrooms, woody vines called **lianas** (LEE-AH-NUHZ), nuts, ants, termites, and the occasional bird's egg or small mammal. They also sometimes eat soil to get nutrients not found in their other foods.

An orangutan's strong jaws and teeth can tear and grind fruit, bark, and nuts easily. They also use their rubbery lips to delicately peel fruit.

Orangutans spend
up to six hours each
day looking for food.

An adult male comes down from the trees to eat a mango. Fleshy fruits make up more than half of the food an orangutan eats.

Finding Food

In the rain forest, different types of trees bear fruit at different times of the year. And some trees produce fruit once a year, while other trees might only produce fruit once every 25 years! When a tree does produce fruit, it might ripen very quickly before becoming rotten. Finding ripe fruit in the rain forest can be hard work for orangutans. As a result, they spend several hours a day looking for food.

Luckily, orangutans have an excellent memory and can recall with amazing accuracy the whereabouts of particular fruit trees and when they bear fruit. Each day, orangutans plan their route through the forest carefully, traveling from one fruiting tree to the next. Youngsters learn these very same routes from their mother.

If an orangutan finds a tree with an enormous crop of fruit, it will spend the whole day there, gorging itself and taking naps.

Using Tools

How does a human get honey out of a pot? With a spoon of course! Sumatran orangutans use a similar method to take honey from a beehive. They break sticks into just the right shape to poke into the nest. They also break open fruit with specially shaped sticks and curl leaves into cups to drink water.

These examples of tool use show how clever orangutans are. Previously, scientists thought that only chimpanzees and humans were capable of making tools. Today, many scientists believe that orangutans are smarter than chimps.

Orangutan Senses

Not only are orangutans smart, they also have excellent eyesight and hearing. Their forward-facing eyes can judge distances well, which is useful when swinging through the trees. They can see colors, too, which is helpful for spotting fruit in the trees. Their night vision isn't very good, though. Fortunately, that's not a problem because orangutans tend to sleep through the night.

An orangutan's small round ears easily detect the calls and screeches of other orangutans. That is useful if they need to find one another in the dense forest. Their sharp hearing is also useful for detecting **predators**. Orangutans have a poor sense of smell. No wonder the foul-smelling durian fruit does not bother them!

A mother orangutan grips a liana with her long hand. Her playful baby grips the same vine with its handlike foot.

Facing Facts

Perhaps the most striking thing about an orangutan is its highly expressive face. Many people think that of all the nonhuman apes, orangutans look the most like humans. At first glance, orangutans all look similar. However, they actually have very individual facial features and their expressions vary a lot—just like humans.

It's easy to tell Bornean and Sumatran orangutans apart by looking at their faces. Sumatran orangutans have long, oval faces. Bornean orangutans have much wider faces. Also, Sumatran males have bigger mustaches and beards than Bornean males.

Both Bornean and Sumatran males have very fat cheeks. However, the Bornean's fleshy cheeks can grow to be so huge that the orangutan has difficulty seeing around them!

With its wrinkled face and beard, a baby orangutan looks a little like an elderly human!

29

When food is scarce, a male orangutan can use the fat in its cheeks to help it survive until other food becomes available.

Cheeky Cheeky

Why do male orangutans have such fat cheeks? No one knows for sure, but some scientists think that these fleshy flaps may make a male orangutan more attractive to females. An orangutan with big cheeks might look more threatening, too, which is useful for scaring off other males.

Both male and female adult orangutans have throat sacs. These sacs increase the loudness of the calls that orangutans make to one another across the forest. Males have particularly large sacs that they can blow up like huge balloons. They then release the air slowly from the sacs, and the result is a loud bellow.

The Long Call

Once in a while, the hum of the rain forest is interrupted by the "**long call**" of a male orangutan. This extraordinary noise begins with a low rumble that gradually turns into a deafening hoot similar to an elephant's trumpet. It then finishes with a series of burbling sighs. It usually lasts two to four minutes.

Orangutans mainly use the long call to warn other males to keep out of their home range, or **territory**. It might also be used to find other orangutans in the area. Some scientists think that males may use it to attract females, too. A local story from Borneo says the long call is a cry of pain. In the story, the cry is made by a distressed orangutan when he discovers that his human bride has been captured.

The long call is so loud that it can be heard at least two-thirds of a mile (1 km) away.

An 11-year-old Sumatran male bears his teeth in an aggressive display.

No Trespassing!

Male orangutans move through the forest in territories of about 2 square miles (5 sq km). These areas overlap at the borders with the territories of several other males. Several females and their young usually live within this area, in smaller overlapping ranges. Females claim an area just big enough to feed themselves and their **offspring**—about 250 acres (100 ha) each. Male orangutans, however, prefer a larger area, so they can find **mates** as well as food.

A male orangutan makes long calls to identify himself as the owner of his territory. If that fails to keep away a male intruder, he makes a "**display**." A display is a noisy performance intended to scare an unwelcome guest away. A territorial male makes a display by shaking and throwing branches furiously while screeching loudly. This tactic usually works. Occasionally, male orangutans fight. They do that on the ground. Most fights occur because the intruder wants to mate with one of the females whose home range lies within the territory.

Slow Breeders

Orangutans are slow-growing, slow-breeding animals with a long life span. A wild female is first ready to mate at about ten years old, but she does not usually begin to have babies until she is 15 years old. After giving birth, she will not mate again until she is more or less finished raising her young. That generally takes about four to eight years. As a result, the orangutan population grows very slowly. A female orangutan raises at most four young in her 45-year life span.

Males are also ready to mate at ten years old, but they often have to wait a few more years to mature and become attractive to females. During this time—which varies between 8 and 20 years—most males become bigger. They learn how to make the long call and they grow long, shaggy hair. They also need to have fought for and won their own territory.

Bornean male orangutans spend more time on the ground than Sumatran males. That might be because tigers—which will attack orangutans—no longer live in Borneo!

A Sumatran baby orangutan clings tightly to its mother as she swings from tree to tree, looking for food.

Tiny Baby

Female orangutans usually mate with the strongest male they can find. The pair might stay together anywhere from a few days to a few weeks before going their separate ways. Eight to nine months after mating, the female gives birth to a baby in her nest. The newborn weighs about 3 pounds (1.5 kg), less than half the weight of an average newborn human. Rarely, a mother gives birth to twins.

A newborn orangutan usually has a little moon-shaped face and a spiky orange coat of fur. Its little brown face has lighter areas around its eyes and mouth, which darken as it grows older. The mother **nurses** her baby with milk. She and her youngster stay in the nest until the baby is old enough to travel—usually after just one week.

Motherly Love

Female orangutans make great mothers. They love to cuddle and tickle their young ones, and are fiercely protective. Sometimes, they play games like hide-and-seek with their baby. An orangutan mother keeps her baby's fingernails short by cutting them with her teeth. And she washes her baby's coat with rainwater!

A baby orangutan is completely dependent on its mother for at least the first three years of its life. For the first year and a half, the baby hangs onto its mother's fur almost all the time. The young orangutan nurses for about three years. After this period, the youngster usually stays around for another three to four years, sleeping in the same nest as its mother and learning how to survive in the rain forest.

An orangutan mother is very protective of her baby.

41

This young orangutan has started to learn to grasp onto branches as it travels through the forest with its mother.

Just Like Us?

Orangutan babies have a lot in common with human babies. As well as being tiny, both human and orangutan tots cry when they are hungry or uncomfortable. They love affection from their mother, too. Often, a mother and baby can be spotted cuddling and nuzzling each other. Like humans, baby orangutans show many emotions, such as sadness, happiness, and anger.

But there are important differences between human and orangutan babies. Human babies are eager to learn language and also love playing with toys. Orangutan babies do not have these characteristics.

A Lot to Learn

Growing orangutans will learn everything they need to know from their mother. First, the mother shows her offspring what is good to eat and what is not. One of the most important things a mother teaches her baby is the best travel routes through the rain forest to find food. She will show her youngster how to climb and swing from tree to tree. She does that by pushing her little one onto a branch. It then has no choice but to learn how to come back to her on its own. It's scary at first, but after a lot of trying, climbing becomes second nature to the baby.

Other important skills include learning how to build a nest and recognizing predators, such as clouded leopards and—in Sumatra—tigers.

At the age of four years, a young orangutan is able to choose its own food, swing through the trees, and make a nest. However, it still likes to cuddle up to its mother at night.

One reason orangutans live in trees is to avoid predators, such as this Sumatran tiger!

Although adults rarely interact, young orangutans love to play together.

Growing Up

When a female orangutan gives birth to another baby, it is the time for the older youngster to leave the family nest. It's tough at first, and often the young orangutan will try to jump back in. But, the mother won't put up with that. She will even resort to smacking her older offspring if it doesn't obey orders.

Eventually the youngster starts building its own nest, but it stays close to its mother and the new baby. Young orangutans love to tickle and play with babies—some have been seen playing peek-a-boo. Soon, the older youngster starts to feel more independent. It might even begin to hang out with other **adolescent** orangutans. At some point, the adolescent will wander off, often with others its age. Eventually, the young orangutans will most likely live alone.

Difficult Times

Once there were millions of orangutans in Asia. Today, mostly due to human activity, their **range** is restricted to two islands and there are only about 40,000 left in the wild. Unfortunately, the future for the orangutan looks bleak due to destruction of their **habitat** and the pet trade.

Humans are cutting down the rain forest for wood. The wood is made into furniture and sold to people in western countries, including the United States. Without the forest, orangutans have nowhere to live. Fortunately, logging is now illegal in some areas.

Other people capture baby orangutans to sell as pets or zoo animals. Often, the mother is killed in order to catch the baby. The young animal is then packed into a small box and shipped to a faraway place, usually in bad conditions with no food or light. Most of the stolen babies die. Thankfully, the authorities in Sumatra and Borneo are clamping down on this illegal activity. That offers hope that orangutans will continue to survive in the wild for many years to come.

Words to Know

Adolescent   A young orangutan between the ages of five and eight years.

Arboreal   Living in trees.

Display   A noisy performance by a male ape intended to scare away other males.

Durian   A pleasant-tasting, but very smelly, fruit that orangutans eat.

Great apes   Any member of the family Hominidae, which includes orangutans, chimpanzees, gorillas, and humans.

Grooming   Cleaning, tidying, and brushing hair.

Habitat   A type of place that an animal or plant lives in. Forests, grasslands, and lakes are all types of habitats.

In captivity   A term that refers to animals living in a zoo or with humans.

Lianas   Woody vines that orangutans eat and use to swing on.

Long call   A loud cry made by male orangutans. It can last up to four minutes.

Mates	Animals that breed.
Nurses	Drinks milk produced by the mother.
Offspring	The young of an animal.
Predators	Animals that hunt other animals.
Rain forest	Densely forested area that is hot and rainy. At least 8 feet (2.4 m) of rain falls each year in the rain forest.
Range	The region in which a certain type of animal is found.
Sign language	Using movements of the hands and arms to communicate.
Species	The scientific word for animals of the same type that breed together.
Territory	An area that an animal lives and feeds in and often defends from other animals of the same kind.

Find Out More

Books

Harkrader, L. *The Orangutan*. Endangered and
Threatened Animals. Berkeley Heights, New Jersey:
Myreportlinks.com, 2005.

Orme, H. *Orangutans in Danger*. Wildlife Survival. New
York: Bearport Publishing, 2006.

Web sites

All About Orangutans
www.enchantedlearning.com/subjects/apes/orangutan/
A lot of facts about orangutans, with links to a picture to
print and color in and a quiz.

Creature Feature: Orangutans
www.nationalgeographic.com/kids/creature_feature/0102/
orangutans2.html
Fun facts about orangutans.

Index